CITY
ECLOGUE

Ed Roberson

a t e l o s

2 3

ISBN 978-1-891190-23-0
First edition, fourth printing

Ŧ Atelos

A Project of Hip's Road
Editors: Lyn Hejinian and Travis Ortiz
Design: Lyn Hejinian
Cover Design: Ree Katrak/Great Bay Graphics

City Eclogue

Contents

City Eclogue

Beauty's Standing

The Open

Ornithologies

Her Movement Buried By The Moment In Occurrence

Eclogue

City Eclogue

Stand-In Invocation

One of your clairvoyances who could've
seen her way to speak   stared clearance through.
A New York scoping out instead of eye
contact.   No voice or vision, no called muse —

one of your sightings that would be a dream
if it cared, if it loved you more, kept you
awake asleep and fucked you woke with your eyes
rested in the open beyond what's seen.

No. One more of the feeling un-invoked
spoken out of these days' put you through
proofs before granting you speech   testifies
she is not the mouth of anything you wrote

these days.   ould've
                                                   ould've.

She knows the form, her tongue's just sharp and short of.

City Eclogue: Words for It

Beautifully flowering trees you'd expect
should rise from seeds whose fluttering to the ground
is the bird's delicate alight
or the soft petal stepping its image
into the soil
                      but here come the city's trucks
bumping up over the curb dropping
the tight balls of roots in a blueprint out
on the actual site in the street
someone come behind with a shovel will bury.

City of words we're not supposed to use
Where everyone is lying when it's said these words
are not accurate, that this shit is not the flowering,
that shit off the truck and not the gut
bless of bird and animal dropping isn't somehow

just as natural a distribution
as the wild bloom   The trees are
delivered in ordered speech   as is
dirt mouth curse and graffiti
to where the backed perches want them.   Bought with
                      the experience that thought up city.

The idea of the place
tramples up its rich regenerate head
of crazy mud into the mutant's changling potion.
Committee cleanliness and its neat
districts for making nice nice and for making sin
may separate its pick of celebrant monsters;
                      but which it is now is
irrelevant as the numbered street sequence
to archival orders of drifting sand.
What it will be   the stinking flower
the difficult fruit   bitter   complex   the trunk   — all

              on the clock   on the tree rings' clock
              history's   section cross cut
              portrait   landscape
                                  it already
              knows   composts into ours the
                                  grounds for city.

Sequoia sempervirens

We are about what   a squirrel's size
is to a tree   to this tree

we are the miles as shoe to
city limits   one line

we rip around
getting our nut

        off   to the city

Foot totals map   ply upward
impossible city on top of

city even down   underground
layered into time

it seems to

have grown from our gotten
nut   the fruits of a pleasure in

lifting our scale into the scale
of a weight we feel   we're part of

into this other dish we can feel
rest into balance

our nature in nature nature
in us

The long stabilized climate   the fattening

of an abundant season
the people pack on

into a city;
venerable aging of the gather

into the fold's royal robe   venerable aging
of the met crowd into community;

the self destructions squirreled away in what grows

Settled.

But we seem almost a fire dependent
species like this tree

one that grows around fire
as if burn   were a wire fence   a post

of imbedded iron   a piece of shot
a plate in our heads

for the guest lightning.

The Distant Stars As Paparazzi

the News   cattlebirds of paper fly around
thinking   a movie shot
and not that they're just rubbish light enough
and it's time for pick up

which will dump them into dance with garbage gulls
who partner themselves
with popular images   pages flying
winged magazines.

the humped earth settles up to its horns in mud
roaring   then bubbles
of going under cloud air with odor —
stink also a local character

a spirit   flocking its natural herd decompositions
along a mound made into natural
ground for later   their coats sheared into compost for
the spin
into garden earth.

Naked, the planet turns itself
into itself   a mirror
modeling beautiful   it shows its timeless line
for season in its fashion

As it crested the hill

The street as it crested the hill,
the buildings on each side   the railings
of a moon bridge,

crossed over
the weight and flowing of the earth. As if
within a palm's casual brush

swept up into the hanging raceme blossoms —
the white clouds.
Filming a chase,

the crew's stunt men
must aim   the car's lift into the air
for the picture.

Just more vegetation
in a visual garden of curves, bridges, of hills
in the streets

to stroll over within its hour, its season
of arc. The fields,
theaters,

battle arenas and park
lands of nomad circuitry fill the air
with booming then they empty.

Someone always walks
the track of the coaster before opening,
thinking it out

way ahead,
that walk winds
up the best ride.

The cross streets step down;
but from the crest of the hill, the scenic
overlooks, the cliffs

ledges,   whether momentum
enough to lift or the stepping out wish
troll beneath,   there is a push

from high places
— not translated as yet at happening
as fly or jump —

disguised as gravity.
Ecstatics who wear no mask of surface
for the soles of their feet

steer into the air
their burning steps   losing sight
of the hand held out by the sun

lose orbit
and its turning dance
track of days.

Ra   whose rays
once ended in open hands   today is
fingers walking in me

the meditations of this labyrinth
this ride before the opening push
into what critical mass the hours bring.

The best ride on gravity is walking.
Only the densities
of distance and destination

suck you over its edges,
its horizon,
until you can't be seen any more simply as

a single human ability, only
collapsed   a whole system
firing its jet emergent out

into space   that shot   a step only as much
as the ability to bring it down
to its feet

               scale   legend   map
the way the earth comes gliding
The Way Earth   comes gliding

Sit In What City We're In

1

Someone may want
to know one day how many steps we took
            to cross one of our streets,
to know there were hundreds
in one city   streets in one direction
           and as many
as could fit between the land's contours
crossing those,
            our hive grid as plumb
as circles flanked into the insect
hexagonals,
           our stone our steel.

Others may want more
to know what steps aside the southern streets required
           to flow at last free to clear,
to know how those kept out
set foot inside, sat down, and how
           the mirrors around the lunch counter
reflected the face
to face — the cross-mirrored depth reached

                        infinitely back into either —
the one pouring the bowl over the head of
the one sitting in
                        at that counter

                        this regression this seen stepped
back into nothing both ways
From which all those versions of the once felt sovereign
                        self   locked together in the mirror's
march from deep caves of long alike   march back
into the necessary   together
                        living   we are
reflected in the face to face we are
a nation facing ourselves our back turned
                        on ourselves   how
that reflection sat in demonstration
of   each face
                        mirror reflecting into mirror generates

a street cobbled of the heads of
our one
                        long likeness
the infinite regressions.
The oceans, themselves one,   catch their image

                    hosed by riot cops down the gutter into
The sphere surface
river

                    looked into   reflects
                    one face.

2

A here and not-here division of things,
where the future is in the same
                        place as the past, is
maybe one of the African
masquerades of time   like these facing mirrors
                        in which time is making faces
at you from the elemental
moment,   the faced and yet to be
                        faced
in one frame   where from, where to are faces of here.
Where a few in the crowd at that lunch counter
                        face their actions.

Where what dark is revealed
in the face to face   is a back to back.
                        The words of that god
against us. In the glass, the face
observed, changes the looking at that face, cancels both
                        their gaze to transparence, opens
around it a window containing right here
around us;   and in that window these
                        same
— in the lapped frame of this one moment —
are the other one's
                        world we see into in ours:

You can't smash the mirror   there but it break here.
And in it you see   that you can't see
                    your own back,
your angel of the unfamiliar, of that not like
your face... See.   and
                    relax that hand raised against
your impossible
hand   that reaches to give the pat, to okay   touch you
                    at the unfamiliar, those stubs of your
back.

3

From mirror to window   glass   to thin air
between   and finally, us with no you nor I
                    but being
— with all our world —   inside the other;
but there only in   our each part yet having
                    no displacement of the other,
just as each wishes   the self not lost, shared
being in common in each other   being
                    as different as
night and day still   of one spin.
The sphere surface
                    of this river.

To know ourselves as a god would know us
would make us gods
                    of ourselves   we are so
fused in communication we happen at once,
as if as one   gazing
                    ball pivot of critical gardens,
cocked Creations.   Here, in the glass of the city,
a godlike simply knowing doesn't determine
                    what built
raft of citizen draughts where the street runs
up the walk to the door   ocean teased apart
                    to its each drop

of rain.
Someone is riding a bus, too tired
for everything   except what is right;
                a god has his back against the wall
of a church in Birmingham;
the marchers take to the streets.
                Someone may want to know
what city we're in
that curves glowing over the edge
                into an earth.

Place Lit By A Window

Naked socket hanging from the ceiling,
a sperm shape,   the wire, a tail;
the head   without the light screwed in knows

somewhere between the four crack walls
and trash deep stair-less floor that   a common place
hope expects there to be

some bootstrap an egg slips from
from which the president of something
or other always a dawn will come.

Watching too much sunrise warms the breast
but often clouds the hands'
emptiness and the pocket you're not facing

up to that   likes the day moving in this direction
and invests
in more ice cream for when you turn to leave

to hope you on your way.
Pockets knows there's no guarantee you'll see
the morning but your journey pays

                his way.

                *

*

The blinding that misheld belief inflicts
— like the torch held backwards that burns the dark
into your eyes   and for its moment all direction

instead become expectation —   leads
someone else out of the bind of your being
held up for his hope he can get away

with this if one or two of you do too:
if even one colored overcomes
this darkness   that's enough light to continue

naming this conceit an exemplar   what is expediency.
While inside   the dark adapted eye
can see what shapes   what little light decides,

can read where walls write up a room from,
and   from where it looks,   see the outside
see to dress in the dark   know when the train is

leaving   and see its way underground
to the station. One car on time is nowhere   it knows
the whole city has to get where it's going.

*

*

Of what we see,
our own clearness is the handle end
of that light. The real proportion   the real numbers of
obscurity to bootstrap apply   only to sample blocks:
             in only the sufficient number do matters
             of chance become one of certainty,

an observation that secures the group   not any one
individual.   You author your own maze's
manual   its figure out   its guided eye.

             In the role of the beloved   the window
             screens its legend portrait of the city
on the blocks   It's your own program of cells
for you to look out of a life-size frame at —
you walk your own   portrait —
             your own city   not a mark to have to toe.

Way inside,

the window less a window —
a gray opalescent dirt shade
of a light fixture:

the city on the wall
all cities have of themselves framed in mind
matted with the room

in question —   A subway map.
Yet a more honest expectation,   a time
schedule of arrivals mapped as view,   a flat answer
                                          on the wall
          for light.

Beauty's Standing

Only eye lives in this
no place anything else can
    come to rest on

Chairs sit in visual positions
proposing your sight
    on the room as beautiful

That this is his only
company for conversation
    he gets

A room physically
Functionless   answers
    the silence flatters.

People talking to pictures
in a magazine culture live on walls
    flatter than ground

Dailies of something missing
rip pages out of them to bundle
    with sharp wire and send

back to them unread
for pulp   to caulk
    the hole in such pockets.

A practical place to sit
cities   cites the always where
       cities have been

the eye looks out
for this from this
       seating together

Beauty's Standing

1

The buildings stood, a bunch of
garbage odd-sized barges

lashed together between the currents
of the railroad and river, scuttled

sinking upend into an oily sky,

they are made   into land people pour into
to colonize   as artificial reef is

sunk next to dying corals
on the sea floor   such housing.

Something is off

re: the water   the heat
is out of control   the land toxic.

Building up more junk on more
junk   doesn't pay the bills & get the light back on

2

The flesh form of the city doesn't move
in the same time as the city's material
forms move into era and monument.

The lovely women styled in as no other
time are not the body of this space they make
only the flow through it.   And all

this to river deep into and shape
the city   rosetta stone   the populace
pours in   An ocean   each say moving
its grain at its one time.   The corners smooth

into their large design   a Times
or a Washington Square   a park
of the highest form of pickup
basketball in The Village a Harlem sound —

and like that sound from which musics are made,
the day's whole city of words is not the language.

The kind of walk that's always taking cover
instead of steps   that gets to the corner
and can see what's around it by the faced
direction targets cite the shooter placed,

by where people look for what's against them,
we slouch that walk   eye on our government
without thinking   because we can't think
without our common term yet   just a stink

of sense that something's wrong here we always
used the word for   about our enemies:
dictatorship,   takeovers,   military
class rule,   compromised legitimacies

These words hide   as understood   our denial of such
with exclusive meaning   by definition never the us

or) By

our self-referent definition   none of these words
admits us and are   (still in our habit   Colored Only.

3

Oceans through the crosswalk   dipping a step
out of each of the dances   of languages
crossed from —

        the steal away, less noticed than   wept,
the run for it, that sometimes made   it, turns on
a permanent state

                of flight, feet touching and not
ever a possible ground,
spun off   all that is earth   all harborage.
                                                Oceans
                        through the crosswalk
boil down   to a martial art people do —
a perfected stance of fight   walked

                                talked
hands eddy around a point
poked into the air   Each scythe and its heaven declare —

        The maelstrom we had all outrun
        dances us   right here.

4

That powerful level of segregationists
the civil rights movement never reached

never guilty or active agent within
the necessarily narrow focus needed to pin

never guilty of any more obvious
than wanting things this way,

the great weigh of wealth's want
that moves other men's hands

and feet and leaves its own clean,
the weight that never touches

anything but is carried
into the place it is always preparing

for itself above all movements,
into presidencies, oligarchies. These.

---

i.e., platform language

Family values were always a disguise
to hide the value a following had

to the families positioned to live outside
values not profitable

to their Olympiad —   despite the toll —
values = mere votes for their pull.

5

(is ' im thux-ed fa we)

the street-talk birdcall of sucked teeth,
is disgust it   flicks its feathers
           to tighten even more sleek
and rotates its face completely away   — the owl —

when there is mention of their leader, their gods?
Athena? no one but a name for newborn
girls, like dot ellipse dot dash not serious.
          Remember dot dot did dit dot dot dash?

did it it did and returns still a call
for some same coattail pulling this enough
to make shit stop, make it change up
for some better call for all a us

and make it stick, not someone come back
three years later and shoots it down in the house.

What fathers
of their country and of following

fathers in
half the moral values bunch have been

arrested for what they mouthed
off against

but done themselves done
as in   What kind of really bastard son

wishes his father had won
election to eradicate his sister

for the fucker's birthday?
Immaculate Christians still conceived

in.   believed in
office   their sin washed away.

6

(the first casualty is where you live)

The quiet of the house evacuates into the street
leaves all the rooms to follow the haunting

concern without yet subject   the ghost with its candle
floats across the walls red revolving patrol

lights a spun radiant weapon a night-
stick elucidation   a beating without a given reason

that just shows up at a door
in the neighborhood   just happen

to be
Who this time

Outside on the street   look back inside
our own windows

see the red shadow of the ghost crossing the walls
where we live

7

(there was no gun)

we blink our eyes at any sudden loud noise,
this probably wipes the eyes to see more clearly

did he see forty-one times   the forty-one shots
end his life in forty-one deaths in time

to understand what he already knew about black
people looking like to whites with guns

not thinking   did their eyes open at the sound
forty-one times clearing at forty-one

glances at chances to blink getting away?
wrong about what to keep from getting away

we blink our eyes to erase what we see
or to clear the eyes to see what we don't

believe we're seeing   thoroughly enough
to be exact at what   held no gun to be forgot

I need to get in here   and say
I need to get in here   a place
I need to get in   I need a place if only for the night left
                                             to stay
and say some things   about how much time
we got to come up   we got
to   we got
with   nothin' left
                              listen up   nothin'

8   *(the collection)*

I'm awakened thinking of men running
after the truck after   maybe hearing

them throw their bags on   their boxes cans garbage
one after the other   (& abt their papers

grabbed up onto the truck.   Their refugee
or here employed status —

the worksong sound of their holler clears up.
Except I've dreamt a border hours ahead

of myself.   What's left after the night-scream
brake and start   I have to bring in in the morning.

I know there is a pick-up schedule
for the hearse just as for the garbage. I just don't get it

in my box with the borough junk mail dropped off
explaining only to be thrown back for collection.

I only get the notices for those
I have to lose — leave —   turning to the curb.

Someone setting the recycling out tonight has let
loose a tumbleweed of trash and loud plastic

bottle drumming curb to curb across the floor.
I don't know what dance this is   what song

has been called   Only that the forecast tonight
is arrived   a high wind —

A dance
to chance to come around again together as

or the dance a seizure of fear
shoulders like a rider   and possesses with that

terror mobility: Everything runs
for the match speed it needs to jump on.

The rhythm of the braking and acceleration sings
its squeak from the hog-mouth wheel: there is no real
                                                    stopping.

9

The other side of the idea
of having anything
to throw away to be collected is *après*
the collections —

is our territory
After empties us
out into the local dump
to turn what we can find over

to make up
into something we can use. The catch
up   in what
we catch off the truck.

That we should catch up
or make up any losses is the floor
the union boss wants
for his house

for him for who's
gonna get paid

and twice to put it in
for the vote to

stay ahead
of the niggers
of all colors other than.
And they say God

this is a great   countryland
of opportunity! Get me

a piece of that
fall off the back of a truck   first
                              economy
I can pick up like
Y' know, with the bootstraps!

10

he woke in a fight for his life   in that
he went at the alarm clock as if to kill
before that something about waking killed him

a terror only when over was he aware
his heart racing   and his first sense of time
the few seconds of panting before his head pounds

as though his days could beat him before they dawned
and disappear into broad daylight as the way things are
run around here.

"It's nothin' but a bunch of little guys
with all their dough tied up in raggedy trucks
ain't makin' no money. We can take that. Cut the niggers' tires…"

the city subcontracts   with the mob.
Brakes howling wild as a thing possessed
loose in the alleys, the city's garbage truck

lopes house to house, street to street, the wolf —
in that hour before light —   to the sleepless.
It has our scent. It has our fucking jobs.

when the city tore down   like shooting
all the houses living   on our street

we couldn't even get the job
of hauling

away
our dead

Height and Deep Song

Pulled by the full disaster's view or thrown
upward to the look-out's level
                crying

from that ledge   the song of what it comes
down to
                but unable to jump strapped in

with the wonder the words can come up with
stripped   in the scramble of birth spill —
                the speechless

cover binding
the know this
                on the spine

the body arrives screaming   written
all over it

                what breath is
                then writing

more of

The Open

The Open

Their buildings razed.   they ghosts
    their color that haze of plaster dust

their blocks of bulldozed air opened to light
    take your breath as much

by this kind of blinding choke as by the loss felt
    in the openness

suddenly able to see
    as if across a drained lake from below

a missing surface: the knowing   everyone
    by some common

immersion schooling you   not drowned in exposure
    the way   the neighborhood

a village packing up and leaving raises you with
    the catch

out in the open.
    Suddenly able to see

            People lived where it weren't open,

a people whose any beginning is disbursed
    by a vagrant progress,

whose any settlement
    is overturned for the better

of a highway through to someone else's
    possibility.

A people within a people   yet whose link
    we lived in a distant separation as if

across the low valley we never knew
    our ward flowed through

or knew the downtown was as close to
    as the gold dome on the new municipal

horizon.

        From the project slabs leveled
to the poor pride-kept and neat
    stands of

old houses mowed down
    to vacant lots of garbage lawn,

the fallowing lies there
    invested in waiting for

the dead to clear   and the air
        to smell of the scrub of money   and more

having seeded out the running into
        a new running from,

those with money enough to hold and time
        retain

— over even the well-off only a generation —
        their run of the country.

*

Our plot changed,   its figure
     the decades the same phone   number rolls over

the family migrant memorizations   get zero
     calling back   as much as feel

the zero open   its mouth as much as overwrite
     all entry from now

on   our black books addressing the country where
     you spoke our name and turned   as plowed earth up as

by a glacier   as by erasure changed to this
     house of dead connection of no warm answering

on the lines
     held frozen in our hands.

               Word is
that walking
     plots meaning from the chaos of point,

in that,   movement is line   of body marking off
     the been   place's journey into story.

So in the hands of our high ground   we set out
    for the capitols, the major passes   through the storm

to speak up   though we knew
    we could end as that

body on the run-off tongue
    of the glacier: silent

unremittingly possible   spirit of
    a story   unrestrained by known beginning with

ways remapped,   these streets,
    their

nothing put up in the place of   there
    not even a place anymore

can't even walk it as
    a street!   history plotted by a strewn line of

curbstone   rubbed out down
    to a rock flour: Ghosts

their color that haze of

*

..our North American stele,
    the silo's flashpoint cloud

of the fine segregations
    taken as a core from our society,

reads like the streets, the history
    of mine shafts, mills   moments before blowing

the chamber,   core layers of color   line counting off
    under the pressure.

..of water   fire
    hoses

run people off down the pavement   each
    one the iconic light

-ning) in the cloud

of wakening to the tv's black and white
    camera   impossible spontaneous

possible phoenix re-invention
    of the nation that year.

The whole column
    from top to bottom open   as if

it were the strangled neck
    of the hourglass that was going up

and not its falling sands:
    as if all our chance.   seconded.   grace

God's strange rope spinning things open out of sky,
    up in smoke

our tornado   our lynched
    black pillar of light.

12

In a flattened sea of housing brick rubble,
a catch of broken glass shoots back the light
that lit its flash, a wave's facet, sudden
ember through   full daylight, pierced afternoon
of vacant block after block
                              street
whose lighthouse stare no longer gone looking
for work even as sight to see, flounders
for landing left to its address   and on
those work commutes is sailed past unseen as
someone
                  standing in the last building standing,
in a bare window, barely in his shorts;
his as   none of the windows is curtained nor show
any sign but him of habitation —
the doors off the building, panes gone from
the frames —
                      but him on the upper floor just wakened,
standing there, late foot on the sill as if
balanced on the prow   of his ghost ship he
hasn't even had to take over,
he,
      a lone survivor, a squatter keeping it
open
drifts out into the open

Beauty's Standing (II)

It has   of those decorators' centuries
that hollowness,   that emptiness that who

all this was for don' sit here,   is not
here   and this is, whatever it is

A people's time as a chair;   their hunger —
a bowl, an ornate dinnerware;   the fill —

one piece of unknown use short,   its failure,
by the thousands

of bellies now a currency,
a pattern, a simple handiwork betrayed

I need to get in here   and say
I need to get in here   a place
I need to get in   I need a place if only for the night
left

                                        to stay
and say some things   about how much time
we got to come up   we got
to   we got

                                        nothin' left
                        listen up   nothin'

Destruction is a hidden real investment:
nurture loss in value, mine what's left

to warehouse while it's cheap yet large blocks
beyond the single hand to mouth that needs to hold

those roofs over the packed off mouths' heads
'til all's forgot

               or all's that memory art has
to shape to its default: an auction's lot.

13

.. drifts through a moment left open   the fleet
of them   goes through as if solid was fog
the stone halls of never admit   to selling them

in the waving Sargasso
    of summer heat   smoking
        one man in an upper window bare
foot on the sill   staring
    out a shadowed room hanging out
        of his shorts
across all this
    openness —

        where
when dense with living
    these were close narrow spaces
        streets heaped
with hanging out
    of windows   talk
        three four stories deep
where now you can hear a spill of water at the end
    of what was   a street where someone's come alone
        and opened a hydrant to wash a car

at the curb
    of a vacant lot   an empty field
        or   — if abandoned cars were ships —

at the curb   at the bottom of the sea.
    Chains   the living all have rusted out of
      into ghosts are here
in the dirt   the twisted
    chrome-less tubing of cheap kitchenettes
      the sea-changed sets of everything not worth
a repossession order but worth once all
    they were.
      Worth this   is what they were sold for

14

a scrap of the skin bill still printed with
the address wetted then dried so many times

that as if from sweat or fear   is now
some fiber gone slurried

casts a shape from   of the rubble
a death mask

broken brick   an address
with nowhere the house.

there   if that is a baby's nipple
then this red
tear to pieces of brick

is the buried placenta instinct
a delivery stillborn   from here   from home
born as it's thrown away

Engine

You can experience
the need to leave
                as noise in
an otherwise harmonious
system
                the blues

                the leaving and not
sets up   as a physical chatter
        tear you apart

feel the idling engine of suitcases
trouble the room   break up any image
of a face
                in the mirror   scatter

                over the unpacked slack of surface its
clarity   steal that last nickel
        out of your nature's fact

strip you
down   throw things

into a gear you didn't know would shift

      you can tell
      you runnin'

door open
your work clothes disposition changed
   and the trunk is closed

Standing Strong

He wore the mismatched shoes   he said in style
when one of your boys was gunned   and it could
go either way   and you wanted to say
you were with him step for step still tight.

When I asked what each either of the way
was   he said it wasn't nothing just mismatched
shoes   no more shamanic a dressing up than that
as if he could not see what he sees to

wear   what he seizes on as medicine
from here   from standing strong   canonical
incantation and station of the street
for keeping on   his feet washed by the hands

of black angels of pavement   of dark roads
towelled in lynch linen   basins of shadow.

He wore his mismatch with the dead as night
a night like living sun among these shades
of dragging down   hooked up with even darker;

each star   a stare down a bore of light,
each flare of gunshot bull's-eyed   lights a hole
through the gang of hours   from start to finish of

a life   until that blue blocks out a sky,
the night crimes pile their empty chalked off
figurine prizes into a dawn

   He wants to walk away from this.
                                This rough
odd luck how many in his make up brought
— walking away from rope   irons   the capture —
up through him
                     his hair   the glide to his feet
the tendency to *go fu'thuh* in life Somewhere
a couple decent pair of shoes

Ornithologies

Urban Nature

Neither New Hampshire nor Midwestern farm,
nor the summer home in some Hamptons garden
thing, not that Nature,   not a satori
-al leisure come to terms peel by peel, not that core
whiff of beauty as the spirit. Just a street
pocket park, clean of any smells, simple quiet —
simple quiet not the same as no birds sing,
definitely not the dead of no birds sing:

The bus stop posture in the interval
of nothing coming, a not quite here running
sound underground, sidewalk's grate vibrationless
in open voice, sweet berries ripen in the street
hawk's kiosks. The orange is being flown in
this very moment picked of its origin.

42nd Street's Tunnel

The summer
    tunnel of buckeye trees;

the streetlights   — clouded out
    by the dark thickness of leaves — turn

into Japanese lanterns in
    the close local greens that light turns

into paper shades.   The street is
    those

disappearances which by that lit part
    of their flight made string   string

the afterimages of entering
    into a brighten light of it all about

to begin again.   Surfacing from this
    flash

-back   on the way back to the Lincoln
    Tunnel home   to New Jersey,

I face   down a tunnel of light's leaves
    the marquees

of 42nd lined
    fanned out over the street

in those few minutes so late each night
    the pavement briefly dresses as if empty

in a twenty-four hour city.
    Summer is that density

of leaves   of moths around the maelstrom light,
    those destinies that energize the disk

wafer   which bugs that prey bend to take
    eat before forgiven to their feet find fresh —

meat innocence
    the flesh that plays with fire displays —

that being just off the bus   excites,
    steps up in radiance   and seen, sweeps through

the photoflash doors of the event
    horizon.

The street is those
        Entrances

to tunnels hung in light   blindnesses
        we've all seen before and still not

seen through.

But in this country, what country ass
        hauling his history isn't headed here

to lose it

The flash of polish not substance   brass
        not gold. The gold   on paper moving in the dark

ink   the local brand of night   and day
        chauffers its wealth from sight to hidden site.

Idyll

As numbers

as those closely peopled increase,
certain silences are reached
though topographic in step:
                                                    the more people
the more lidded certain sound

                                        and climbing through
the city graphic as through mountains,
you come upon the number's peaks
                                                    a plaza open
out on silence, a ledge
above ourselves hushed we are
                        lifted to without conscious move.

We can look out on the view
from this height   yet level with it in the awful
                                    of all those people,
those many dropped-here moments

of lives pooled in the flow, their movement
suddenly one,   smoothed
                        to a mirror
they, turned to that stone of skip-lightness,   seem

                        to look into   inside.

Open / *Back Up* *(breadth of field)*

To state for the case of poetry
the most recent open field I've crossed
would have to be the block long park lost
in the midst of the security

of local campus mounted police.
Black people get stopped regularly
to show they have university
I.D. by the ones in cars; the auspice

of the animal mounted doesn't fly.
Really, neither do the comic cops. Nature
life and limb gone through divestiture
of place from point

                     reads to the lie
of open

          breasts of field   Elysian,
nor the narrow badge number of the gun.

Monk's Bird Book

Mourning doves are not owls after a while
away from the city   not because the country
appears of a softer feather   less predatory

      you're thinking a sound more naturally friendly
      less edgy and dangerous than the subway
but because the

city city to city within itself so sharply
details for you   actually walks you through
a training in the amplitudes of form

      after a while that sharpness wipes the smile
the natural had you putting on everything.
Really owls   are so soft   their deadly

     accuracy of flight depending on it
they are all but silent   a recognizable law
nobody says shit you learn   the city

has taught you to pick up on   which wings
bring the disk of their sun for around
your neck each day

        and which take you out;
and that your green act of good is natural
in that it too depends on the weather.

Painting From Science for Hui Ka-Kwong

To all those lovely images
    from ancient poets of their cherry trees,
        the blossoms floating alike

as butterflies arriving,
    we are adding birds
        from a newer way

of seeing, i.e.,
    the little dinosaurs
        return to sit

the epochal seesaw of the bough —
    That thunder
        shower of petal?

To the full sweetness
    of late spring's first ice tea,
        a cube

of lizard song
    scaling tinier
        and tinier at whistling speed,

the wave of
    its overflow

---

the petals and butterflies
out of the corner of your eye

are matters of movement and light
the thunder

lizard and the bird
are a matter of time

out of your mind's,
a cognate order of blossom

One In Its Oldest Body

The trains on time meant other than
the dignity of promptness.
Your broken legs

of the journey all lined up;
a map of ethnic dress up
holds the land

to its words
for getting anywhere
forgetting if a person can

get to be a people;
a god acting like a monkey is left
waiting in his station

his life as
the line   the apparition of
those faces.
               Making.

               The number
of lives

lived in the age of the one
in its oldest body

only amounts to
the living one's disorder at the moment,
one that achieves

their single death
despite the whole march
of this army

                    nothing matters but the quality
of the affection —
in the end — that has carved the trace in the mind
dove sta memoria.

                                        Ezra Pound, Canto 76

(.."where memory lingers.")

Ornithology

The gray gulls jittery like
they come in off the street   line up
at a stop
of water that is the city

reservoir.   The arguing wings
seen across the distance to click
as if over a schedule
they post and change in their perch

patterns   The flipping metal panels
of numbers and letters arrivals and departure

track numbers times and destinations —
the rotations of wings   clicking changes on

the overhead board   The sky-changes   the train
of weathers that come through   for them to take.

The State Bird on the Wall in Trenton Station

Each digit and letter space
flipped through
its panel card of unit or alphabet
and settled into
a letter destination   adds up the name
of a destination
city   a train   or a departure point
and the times
the metal winged panels always flapping
changing
moving later and later   further
and further
away   they had a sound   a flock of tin
birds   taking off.

Cowry She

Cowry, the spirit
    of a many,
        old
cracked lips laughing at
    the worn holes
        of gathering and grab,
the boards of the counting
    game,
        the grain houses, the treasuries, cowry
she likes her
    some gulls;
           like her

they can't stop
    moving   enough
        to be counted either,
gray as money,
    gray and dirty thrown
        around like paper
money   a flyin'

    the grabbers can't imagine
        being let

make it to the ground
        to land   the shock
           when
all the wild spirallings
   collapse

       their wings to one spot
coasting the flat line to a stop
    no air of losses

      Cowry,   thrown bone,
ivory tinkling or old "she doesn't listen"
    turned to   gold burned loose in hands
      from polishing her, alchemy of handling,
is still a shell, and shells
          have their voices
   they deal they game   hands
     up   to their emptiness ways
        they roarin' lips to our ear

Her Movement Buried By The Moment In
Occurrence

A Sampler

Depending   on how the center attends
most closely what is around, she hears

or sees him approach, then feels his weight
take up the loose plank bench left beside her

where she sits, placing her in the balance.
She has levels of smell, some she'll drop

into   below that attention, ape sense
with only the language of chemistries,

others are what he wears gives her   his taste
on sweat's index of   his activities.

All this communication, nothing said.
Nothing is voiced.   The moon embroiders

with its almost texture   the sky, the seen
wears its satiny light over what is there

                                        to say.
But the question, What is there to say? is
never answered, and as you see, Nothing

is not that answer. There is something;
something can be said. There isn't anything

that is not the answer; everything is.
It's just that word is not all the saying.

She is listening for safety to arrive
from him   as his shadow saying those lines to

simply the benign direction of light.
She is feeling her survival take note

on a tissue level, the positive
of fear: he's okay. She remembers once

a silence of commuter stop in a dream,
her hands' attention in that sky on her lap.

Smell of Scratch

The storekeeper smells today
as bad as he did

yesterday   the vinegars
of work that preserve us
he never gets out of.
or rests.

You wonder if it's the lettered sign
or the animal franchise of

the human picked up on the distant wind
the oldest sustenant promise
that pulls you in;
you weigh it as neighborhood

against a foreign corporate
or — least troublesome —   just a convenience.

Fingers smell of scratching   even

on words   the odors
of digestion or chewed
cogitative sweetening;
sweat either
decay or salvation.

The scaling off
skin deposits
its deltas   of dust motes;
our lives   brief scent
evaporate.

Love, what do we have
if I don't have my head in
these clouds?

Simple As One Two

1

who having
    put on the disguise of a disease
        to get the little relief of a day or so

and not been able to get the minute off   him
    to enjoy naked the hour   out of costume
        out of the shell of the office

enters back   cramped in
    to crab crap of worse
        disease   to have
to

---

i

            to act

sick which makes him sick to
    do that to
        justify a basic
back-off need of
    self preservation
        to not do
damage to himself
    when the dumbest animal knows
        when

            to

2

to have the culture

    of petri dish architecture as
        success   grow on you
you have to sit still

    in the air
        conditioning a long time:
a green sloth green

    from the algae
        murals
frescoed on   billboard stagnant motion

    a company's
        catchy logo lotion you
smooth

    thing you on yourself
        thinking the thing you
is definitely you

        you's/use confused

---

ii.

    the glass flash and the metal
        sharp edge as you is
    a paper cut but deeper

Alpine Glow In Magritte Landscapes

Those branches catching the last light
float;

over the darkening,
those lifted peaks;

rose
cloud in an already night
sky:

the light holding on

so
as not to end up as only
in our stars

or never

or only carried out on
the day's   solid ground
before going down

Likewise, the tallest buildings reach out
of the city

out of the grid on which the city sits;
buildings
modulate the blocks

upwards
the city a sky of floors

On a desk   a pixilated screen of   the sky   out the window
stacks flying cubes

of itself
if left hanging

Popular on the floor
of the sky   as a screen saver
the Magritte

painting
carried out as an animation

grounded
as we are in viewing our own hanging as

doors through
the landscape not as stalls.

Spontaneous Supremacies

Then   stepped in out of that hall everyone saw
locked at its far end   what was locked out
out of nowhere   now in   starts in its shit   it wants
everything back.

Small cities   words that no longer count   pears
and all hopeful structure   hair   the water claims
and anything else   the white grab
of egret   catching your

eye
can land on   and the land.   It wants
its edges to not touch the other than it
doesn't already have claim to

or isn't.   mostly it doesn't want what
it isn't as its equal   it in anything.

Point.

The place it is possible to call where
The north magnetic pole used to be

The star relaxing from the pirouette
The tiny waist the starry skirt of night

Spins open 'round   the point on which
She turned the part of north earlier to dance

Are all names for a changed bearing   for time
For where the past won't reach with the present's

Unchanged instructions   with the handed down
The hand doomed to hold what it never meant

To lead where it didn't intend to go
To end where it thought eternity was

Its home   and is for eternity where
It does no good.

Psalm

My hands were Molotov cocktails
and I was pounding on the streets
as on a table   buildings jumped
and lives fell over and shattered,
the blood wine and glass all over the ground
of any social fabric spread
between people   certain dishes
of issue   dropped abruptly and concluded.

Surprised my effect
wakes the reverse of what I dreamed
now   I hate cause.   I hate gravity
I want the hands of anything that holds
off me.   If nothing held true
the way I see   then nothing holds.
I want whatever does or is
if not my way   done away.

God is allowed
to kill for the table
the more dead the more is understood that
to be fed   the ham of your enemy's thigh
the blackened ribs
of your own   is to hate the calves of this meal
as your fullest table.
and to be not filled I hate God I eat my lips
His laurel kiss.

The "State as Body" Aspect of Eunuch Rule

I want to kill for my incapacity
to feel.
      To feel   I feel want as want.   to kill.
I'll be simple.

                 A bodily exchange.

A new body
              made not alive to feel,
for the old one that felt
                    scalpeled away.

It's like sex
            the cherry prize   on the head
a hit
        come from the cartoon stars   a crown
turning like galaxies
                  my life around
my head
        'til I no longer have body
with which to

          want   the crossroad's straddle
of milepost that multiples the earth,

or to feel the nakedness of

                    (stripped back
           to the opening entrance)

                                   driving
in
deeper than union   to power   to creation,

to feel the nakedness

                      of what is
against what isn't   what I am
                         and have
and not this absence I will kill to mate
                              — if even with death.

The Counsel of Birds

An alarm waiting a battery
shoved down its throat for some time now   chirps
from its plastic nest attached to the ceiling,
a hybrid re-birthing   anti-fire strain of phoenix.

Nigeria has a bird whose call sounds
like the busy signal of the telephone
and a snake who hangs it up.   Ecuador has
the Galapagos   who hid the messages.

The risen night sweat up   a pacing fog
of nightmare   dries away to waking.
A beeping sun pecks through the dark,
the orange number in its beak   breaking

due into the vapor molecules of its
missed,   its overage of too late
come morning   thin air   augury's loon
singing its insides out out of sight: a dew.

The dawn meadow of coattail-pull pulls me told
to naked. The nothing new of nothing

permanent all I have on. The crow's scare of skin.
Its cocked and trigger of wing, code figure of birds

exploding to flight   free, screams attention blind,
instruction deaf and dumb   before word is these
are gun fire.   And without enough answers answering
     the alarm is our alarms are not working.

Untitled

Sky walls and white
neoclassical moulding cloud
wedgewood days room
after room   of palace season.

Vacation a blue gown of ocean
a host September like her
not since anyone remembers
seen.

Any fall of palaces seemed
shelved among the porcelain
exhibits of narrower centuries
from this beach.

*

A smoke dust empties the sky
of its blue

as if emptying a building —

a whole other
day clears

Under   a shadowless cloud

Ideas Gray Suits Bowler Hats Baal

Adventure somehow decides to bypass all the already

for future release   I attended the last

a graceful request to the quiet you could sense

a scrappy sharing of their account of the music behind them

notational stirrings of a season slower than temperature

a delicate four days up her husky voice   History

a lesson as wearying as it is perpetual

A pruning   no matter how falsifying   of its real complexity

the lighting always perfect for its becoming extinct

just as soup begins simply and innocently   poor

but the mind is always filled with so many ideas

grey suits and bowler hats lifting silently the last

century   and this

jumping in flames from a roaring height for a fooled god

and this cow disease of long rotted enemies

not babel   people driven mad by the silences

they think into

empty voices empty spaces viciously ancient

idol cow

disease of long rotted enemies

When the Morning Come

This high up always felt like suicide
I felt it in my balls when I looked down
face against the window   a reflex action
of muscle to a sense of danger

It abruptly withdraws the testicles
to safety   It hurts   a cramp in the groin
never quite distinguishing between the nature
of survival and a yearning for it over with ...

never quite sorted out ...
I had that problem, so I ...
But here they are   *come together as one*
(a line from the hymn *"'Bye and 'Bye"*) and not a choice

anymore of jumping   or adjusting to the fire
when the morning come.

Well, bye 'n bye   when the morning come
All the saints — well — get together as one
We will tell the story   how it all begun
We will understand it better bye 'n bye

Escape Training: Instructor's Flying Rappel

I jump backwards off the cliff
to show how it's done:

one   two footsteps hit off the face
of the rock then I land

ninety feet below it takes seconds
the rope sings

its rappel   The voice is a burn
to the touch   the glove

on the hand of the flying arm
as light on the rope as smoke.

What should I teach
what should I say I've taught?

This is an emergency maneuver done
right it'll 've been music once it's sung .

You can't hold a note forever
you run out of breath   you run

out of rope   There's a limit
to all of our maneuvers.   This

one's cut-off is its fall short of the height
as if the rest is hung there for you to jump

as the whole thing was   to jump in the first place
This is the end of the rope.
                              The fire
rather than no hope of rescue —
I know how to do this without a rope

without its sound   without a landing right
or wrong   to

do in the silence of it   this maneuver
pure   I jump backwards off the burning upper floors.

Not Brought Up

Just as a matter of scope it felt
    like that
    was the numbers of people
we wanted justice
    brought down upon —
    that many gone along
keeping silent kept in office for —
    Just the sweep of the complicit terror
    against us —

The lynchings each   of the thousands of
    times it happened
    the whole white town
come down
    to a smoky picnic —   each black
    blackened by the family there is in soot
must have felt that
    magnitude against them   stacked
    high   come down out of the hills

must have felt that
    register   force   the running
    or the blank walk   away
up Broadway or Greenwich
    coated in the white   no longer
    simple ash   ghosts   like a range of that
not brought up

Someone Reaching Through A Window

Someone reaching through a window
to close the shutters: the hands
are key   the hands despite

the aimed direction   land back inside;
the open expansiveness of arms
brought closed by the hands on the latch;
            the diminution,

the reach for not being
there   open to the street.

The blanket pulled up over,

the tucking out from inside;   light
nerve   line   and impulse to hear
pulled in

            out of the wall
— if wall is as interface   part hand
   and part touch,
                        the hold shared —
pulled out of that

connection to
all message of   existence of all
but breathing,

        and breathing itself
felt as a cringe felt
as a panic

———————————————————————————

The Slant Away When the Mind in Thought …

In the maelstrom of the hour
glass

        Only the movement —

the arms went 'round in their circle;
the eye makes the few arc degrees in that
swallowing eddy
                as a slant away
when the mind glances a thought and follows
into that

motion.
        Only the movement —

clock-face when the backlighting blinks off;
wave of birds across where the stars
sink 'round in their circle,
                  the hour deeper,
its heart deeper with the day,   drowned in the light,
pulled through the neck of the glass globe

to globe —
        all movement buried by the moment
in occurrence in time.

Eclogue

Eclogue

I wonder if anyone ever thought
to tell time with them   know where their shadow
tipped on 3 o'clock   which floor   which parking spot
from a window desk   or if they ever
stood completely over their own shade's dot
that moment they had no metered footprint;
a peek-a-boo we now find ticketed
as a before and an after   an either
side of a space the zero pulls into,
its long reserve wheel of nothing there.
Yet here a gnomon of absence bears its shadow
placement on some dial of brevity and cold
about life   about the footprint we may leave
empty of light   empty of even point to it.

Here it's flat and densely packed with people
unlike the empty open of the plain;
here our expanse   the grown over dumpsite
of the meadowlands wetlands or the shore
is corps of engineered   the bulldozer-beetle's
ball of dung shines in it   and somewhere the body
hidden in our shit to fake us innocent...
one of our jokes sometimes   things rise and float.

                                        We in the morning
catch, from the train, in the green garbage runoff,
sight of white herons and the cormorants.
When they're there in the evening, we safely
assume the world hasn't gone anywhere;
a take of bearings   the same the next morning
when we'd see the lit towers on the island
we were headed for   we see now the hour.

From the Jersey side we take a bearing, as
on mountains from the vantage of the plain,
on the towers from the vantage of the
dirt-stiffened, unyielding, tarmac of marsh
grass   gray like steel grayed a vegetable steel
from blur and the exhausts of the turnpike.

Position with regard to surrounding objects
here is unlike in the mountains which give
a bearing even from deep within them, let you
see them from inside their formation.

Climbing to the high plateau of the street
from the subway, we check the peaks downtown
or midtown   skyscrapers for direction.
Walk a few doors up the block   they parallax
eclipsed by the postcard we no more see.

*

There was a deep well lit its entire depth
at noon on the solstice   light without shadow:

so with an in-line position with regard
to the sun   any cast line of shadow

would indicate a curve; the distance between
one and not,   an arc of circumference.

That phrase of the psalm says death's shadow is
as deep as that valley which is our grave;

its length is the same cast everywhere   as deep;
no one's is further from death than another's;

death surrounds us   is our uncurbed circumference.
We map our way with only the bearing

of surrounding life   itself borderless
uncontrolled by the surface of our self.

The bridge towers of the Verrazano
are so far apart they tilt away from
each other on the curve of the earth   factored in.

I wonder if from the distance apart
of the The Towers you could figure that reach
'round of the world with this method of shadow?

The shadow of flesh casts how deep and far
a landscape of perspective?   how round
a circumference enough to fit the living

world   does a single life turning to its labor spin?
Take each story of a building as the radius
of expansion   we make of the earth,

concentric spheres   on Turtle Island,
the hundred ten circumferences go nova

So high a reach of vision set on so short
a perspective   the world on the turtle's back:
at top, the wake of star formation   at base, the animal

god.   the jealous Need.   a stomach
of feet   trying to stand through this.

What can we say of our own that stand
in Newark say   so far adrift from a chance

to wash   that the dirt on her feet cracks
into sores the skin of her soles   and steps her in
one more shit infection she has to kick,

one more occupation of her body by
her monkey rulers she will have to throw off
into space   off her back   burned out but clear

of starring habit.   Of her destroyed sun   say
it endows the landfill   on which to build a
new development   "We are the stuff of stars," Sagan says.

Atelos was founded in 1995 as a project of Hip's Road and is devoted to publishing, under the sign of poetry, writing that challenges conventional, limiting definitions of poetry.

All the works published as part of the Atelos project are commissioned specifically for it, and each is involved in some way with crossing traditional genre boundaries, including, for example, those that would separate theory from practice, poetry from prose, essay from drama, the visual image from the verbal, the literary from the non-literary, and so forth.

The Atelos project when complete will consist of 50 volumes.

The project directors and editors are Lyn Hejinian and Travis Ortiz. The director for text production and design is Travis Ortiz; the director for cover production and design is Ree Katrak.

Atelos (current volumes):

1. *The Literal World*, by Jean Day
2. *Bad History*, by Barrett Watten
3. *True*, by Rae Armantrout
4. *Pamela: A Novel*, by Pamela Lu
5. *Cable Factory 20*, by Lytle Shaw
6. *R-hu*, by Leslie Scalapino
7. *Verisimilitude*, by Hung Q. Tu
8. *Alien Tatters*, by Clark Coolidge
9. *Forthcoming*, by Jalal Toufic
10. *Gardener of Stars*, by Carla Harryman
11. *lighthouse*, by M. Mara-Ann
12. *Some Vague Wife*, by Kathy Lou Schultz
13. *The Crave*, by Kit Robinson

Distributed by:

Small Press Distribution
1341 Seventh Street
Berkeley, California
        94710-1403

Atelos
P O Box 5814
Berkeley, California
        94705-0814

to order from SPD call 510-524-1668 or toll-free 800-869-7553
fax orders to: 510-524-0852
order via e-mail at: orders@spdbooks.org
order online from: www.spdbooks.org

City Eclogue
was printed in an edition of 600 copies
at Thomson-Shore, Inc.
Text design and typesetting by Lyn Hejinian
using AGaramond for the text
and GillSans
for the titles and subtitles.
Cover design by Ree Katrak / Great Bay Graphics.
This third printing of 500 copies was issued
in 2012.
This fourth printing
was done by McNaughton & Gunn.